COVER TO
cover

BI
7 SE
AND

CW00431177

Hebrews

JESUS – SIMPLY THE BEST

CWR

John Houghton

Published 2005 by CWR, Waverley Abbey House, Waverley Lane, Farnham,
Surrey GU9 8EP, UK. Registered Charity No. 294387. Registered Limited
Company No. 1990308. Reprinted 2010, 2011, 2016.

For list of National Distributors, visit www.cwr.org.uk/distributors

Unless otherwise indicated, all Scripture references are from the Holy Bible:
New International Version (NIV), copyright © 1973, 1978, 1984 by the
International Bible Society.

Concept development, editing, design and production by CWR
Cover image: Roger Walker
Printed in the UK by Linney Group

ISBN: 978-1-85345-337-3

Contents

5   Introduction

9   Week 1
Brighter than Angels
Fix your eyes on Jesus

15   Week 2
Greater than Moses
Jesus brings us into true rest

21   Week 3
Surpassing Aaron
Grow up; don't give up!

27   Week 4
New Priesthood, New Covenant
Jesus is the guarantee of a better covenant

33   Week 5
Entering the True Tabernacle
The blood of Christ is the final and perfect offering for our sins

39   Week 6
Keep the Faith
It is really worth persevering in our faith

45   Week 7
Towards Maturity
God lovingly coaches us to maturity by means of our tough times

51   Leader's Notes

Introduction

The letter to the Hebrews is one of the truly great books of the New Testament, focusing as it does on the Person and work of our Lord Jesus Christ. We should approach it with a sense of reverent excitement and expect to grow in our appreciation of Christ our Saviour as we do so. Its theme will stir our hearts to worship and reinforce our determination to persevere in our faith. In spite of difficulties in our circumstances and discouragement in our hearts we will be reassured in our belief that we are on the right track in following Him.

Understanding the message of Hebrews is also a key to unlocking the Old Testament and to discovering how it relates to the New. Those who struggle with Part One of their Bibles, particularly the Law of Moses, should find it much easier to grasp as a consequence of studying this material.

Although traditionally ascribed to the apostle Paul, the author of Hebrews is anonymous and so are the recipients. It lacks the 'I, Paul' signature and the usual personal touches characteristic of Paul's writings. Moreover, the general style of the Greek text is more classical than that of Paul's known letters. Suggestions as to alternative authors have ranged from Priscilla and Aquila through to Luke, Apollos, Barnabas or Silas. What is certain is that the theology is fully compatible with Paul and those associated with him. If not written by the apostle himself, we may reasonably describe it nonetheless as the Paul*ine* letter to the Hebrews and in any case trust the divine inspiration and authenticity of its message.

The title and content indicate that the primary recipients were Jewish Christians, though we should by no means restrict its message to such. We do not know of their whereabouts, but it seems reasonable to suppose that they were a group living in a Jewish quarter, probably in a metropolis such as Rome. Their confessed belief that Jesus of Nazareth was the Messiah had provoked considerable opposition and had led to social exclusion within their cultural group. It may well have meant difficulty in getting work, trading goods or buying necessities. They possibly had been excluded from the local synagogue and had certainly suffered the theft of their possessions. Unsurprisingly, they were finding life hard going and were facing a real temptation to give up or at least to compromise their new-found faith.

It is in this context that we must note the famous and unnecessarily contentious 'warning passages' that punctuate the text. These are strongly worded, but they are designed to save the hearers, not to damn them. Too much ink has been wasted in efforts to fit these passages into pre-existing theological frameworks, rather than seeing them for what they are, which is sound pastoral counsel to people under pressure. For this entire book, with all its great statements concerning the Person and work of Christ, is essentially a pastoral letter to people who need encouragement.

That encouragement comes by the writer focusing our attention on the Son of God. From the opening declarations of His glory through to the closing benediction, God's wonderful grace through Jesus Christ lifts our eyes above the difficulties of our circumstances and the futility of the merely religious life. Jesus is brighter than angels; He is greater than Moses; He surpasses Aaron. He has changed the course of history and launched a brand new era. We enter a far greater reality of worship than our forefathers because of Him. There is really no need to waver. Indeed, this is the one and only path to spiritual maturity and we stand in a long line of those who have walked it.

All of us face problems in life and many of us experience varying degrees of opposition for our beliefs. Much of our media, educational and cultural life is hostile to the faith and we find ourselves often in a minority. This takes its toll on our psyches and makes us prone to discourage-ment if not to giving up the cause. To address this we are invited to the Mount of Transfiguration, not to build our self-protective, self-congratulatory religious edifices, but to heed the One who declared with fatherly pride, 'This is my Son, my choice one, listen to Him.'

WEEK 1

Brighter than Angels

Opening Icebreaker

Many people have encountered what they believe to be angels, or they know others who have. Exchange stories of angelic encounters experienced by members of the group or by those known to them.

Bible Readings

- Hebrews 1:1–2:18
- John 1:1–14
- Colossians 1:15–20
- Psalm 2:7–12

Key verse: 'I will be his Father, and he will be my Son.' (Heb. 1:5)

Focus: Fix your eyes on Jesus

Opening Our Eyes

Hebrews announces the dawn of a new era. Whatever God has said in the past is now superseded by the message of His Son. It is less what the Son says, but more the revelation of the Son Himself. A prophet was the conveyor of a message: the Son is the message.

Jesus is the Heir and the Originator – not only the heir to everything as Psalm 2 indicates, He is also the means by which the entire universe was made in the first place. Yet the Son is no derivative being; as the flame is the radiance of the candle's nature, so the Son is the visible expression of God's glory. He is as exact a representation of God as the seal of a signet ring is in the wax. This is why Jesus could say, 'He who has seen me has seen the Father.'

The Son has solved the age-long human quest – how can we deal with the problem of evil? He has provided purification for sins; reconciliation with God is now open for all. God has honoured this accomplishment by setting His Son at His right hand.

Angels are wonderful beings – the wind of God and the fire of God, they fill heaven and are assigned to serve the heirs of salvation. Yet not even to an archangel has God attributed the title 'Son', and no angel has been invited to sit at His right hand. Nor is the future of the cosmos given to them, for this is the Son's inheritance and, in accord with ancient prophecy, His throne is established eternally.

Now, if an angel appeared and delivered a personal message, as say Gabriel to Mary, we would take it seriously – it would probably change the entire direction of our lives. How much more conscientious should we be when we encounter the Son whom angels worship? If an angelic word is binding, then the word of the Son is even more so and to ignore it is to throw away our entire salvation. For the terms are clear: there is no other name under heaven given among men whereby we must be saved.

We should not doubt the Son. He has lived among us and proclaimed the message of salvation Himself. The eyewitnesses are reliable; they saw the dramatic works of the Holy Spirit for themselves. Trust this man; He whom angels worship became lower than the angels, a humble slave obedient to death – God has granted Him the highest honour and the fullest authority.

Yet if this be so, why are we His followers having such a hard time? Quite evidently not everything agrees with the new government, but do not fix your eyes on the rebels. Look instead to Jesus. He came to His glory through suffering, and He understands what it is like for us. The Son is not indifferent; He has lived here, sharing our humanity. We are His family, true descendants of Abraham delivered from the devil's clutches. For the death of Jesus broke Satan's authority and his power to hold us in bondage to the fear of death.

Our High Priest and our senior Brother is neither callous nor disdainful of our lot but is totally identified with us. Not only has He atoned for our sins, but He continues to help us in our times of testing. Angels may minister to us as God's servants; Jesus ministers to us as His own kith and kin.

Discussion Starters

1. Discuss why God made angels. What are they for?

_____

_____

_____

_____

_____

2. People sometimes have difficulty believing that Jesus is God, or even the Son of God. How do you explain this to a not-yet-believer?

_____

_____

_____

_____

_____

3. The more we discover about the universe the more it raises the need for a Creator. What do you understand by the Son being the means through which the universe was created?

_____

_____

_____

_____

_____

_____

4. We are cautioned about ignoring the voice of the Son. What would you heed most, the voice of an angel or the voice of Jesus?

_____

_____

_____

_____

_____

5. If everything is under the feet of Jesus, why is there so much wrong with the world? How are we encouraged to cope with this?

_____

_____

_____

_____

6. What does it mean when it says, 'Jesus was perfected through suffering', bearing in mind that He never sinned?

_____

_____

_____

_____

7. Describe what it means to be part of God's family.

_____

_____

_____

_____

8. The fear of death has many manifestations. Discuss some of these and the way that Jesus has destroyed the devil's greatest weapon.

_____

_____

_____

_____

9. Jesus identifies with us in our sufferings. What do you think this means and how does it help?

_____

_____

_____

_____

Personal Application

Everyone lives by a message. Most westerners follow the message of evolutionary secular humanism, which replaces God with science and technology, and promises a future where the most important person in the world is Me! Sustained by its own prophets and priests, this is the orthodox faith of our age.

To follow Jesus means singing to a different tune, joining a pilgrim people who base their future hopes on Jesus, and living a different lifestyle. Currently, most of us find that following Jesus puts us in an unpopular minority. But we have encountered the Message Himself and, like the early disciples when given opportunity to leave Jesus, we say, 'Where can we go, for you have the words of eternal life?' Whatever the temptation, it is patent folly to depart the faith because of the voice of mere mortals. It's not even the voice of an angel!

Seeing Jesus in the Scriptures

What mental images do you have of Jesus? Some 'see' a medieval crucifix; for others it is a modern film depiction. Some have personal visions that defy description altogether. The writer of Hebrews says, 'We see Jesus … now crowned with glory and honour.' The apostle John, who had known Jesus better than most during His earthly life, saw Jesus in a heavenly vision – Revelation 1:12–16. The power of the vision was sufficient to stun him! Whatever our mental picture, what matters is that we truly worship Him as the One who humbled Himself, died for our sins, and who is now risen and glorified.

WEEK 2

Greater than Moses

Opening Icebreaker

Ask members of the group to describe their favourite ways of resting and relaxation. How often do they do this?

Bible Readings

- Hebrews 3:1–4:16
- John 1:17–18
- Genesis 2:1–3
- Exodus 20:8–11
- Colossians 1:21–23
- 1 Corinthians 10:1–13

Key verse: 'Today, if you hear his voice, do not harden your hearts.' (Heb. 3:7)

Focus: Jesus brings us into true rest

Opening Our Eyes

Honoured by Jews, Christians and Muslims alike, Moses is one of the great figures of history. His writings – from the creation story to the decalogue – continue to shape and challenge our 21st-century world. His charismatic leadership, visionary statesmanship and legislative skill birthed the nation of Israel and established it as a monotheistic theocracy.

Yet if the bright sphere of angels is subservient to Jesus, so too is the political magnificence of Moses. Jesus is the founder and architect of a greater house – a fact that Moses, faithful prophet that he was, recognised in his own time. Moses built as a servant but Jesus builds as Son and Heir. We are that house, the temple of the Holy Spirit, living stones shaped and cemented together by Jesus Himself.

This process requires our active participation, so we must learn the lessons of history to ensure that we do not, through lack of faith, make the same mistake as others. Those in question were the generation that left Egypt under Moses' leadership. They proved to be disobedient, hardhearted, prone to idolatry, complaining and downright rebellious. Rather than co-operating with God's purpose to bring them into the land of promise, they heeded the doubts of the unbelieving spies and committed themselves to 40 years of desert wandering until all, with the exception of Joshua and Caleb, were dead. Their disobedience of unbelief tested the patience of God to the point that they forfeited His blessing. It is a salutary lesson. We must look after one another to ensure that none of us turns away from the living God with a heart of sinful unbelief. Sin is deceptive and deadly. It is capable of fossilising our souls until we are left without spiritual feelings.

One of the central characteristics of true faith is its sheer perseverance – we must start well, run well and finish well, all the while keeping our eyes fixed on Jesus and encouraging one another to do the same. It is not enough to hear the gospel preached, nor even to believe it. The message has to be mixed with faith; that is, we must act upon it. Faith is a doing word.

The promised land represented rest, settlement, peace and abundance for the people of God. It contrasted starkly with their slavery in Egypt and their wanderings in the wilderness. Because of their unbelief they missed out on that rest. It is a bit like someone being given the tickets for an all-inclusive holiday, but choosing instead to criticise the donor and then refusing to go to the airport because they couldn't be bothered and they believed that it was too good to be true anyway.

The failure of that generation did not end God's intention to offer His people rest. Their children did in due course settle in the land. Yet this points to a greater truth, for there is another place of rest for the people of God. It is an inner condition, a Sabbath for the soul – the peace that comes to those who have ceased from attempting salvation through their own good works and have come instead to trust in the grace of Christ and His saving work on our behalf. This Sabbath rest for the soul has its origin in God's work of creation when on the seventh day He rested from all His labours. We are encouraged to make every effort to enter that inner rest.

Discussion Starters

1. What do you think makes Moses one of the most important men who ever lived? What is his relevance to life today?

_____

_____

_____

_____

_____

2. Discuss what you mean by 'hardness of heart'. What are the symptoms of this spiritual disease?

_____

_____

_____

_____

_____

3. How can we best encourage one another to continue in the faith?

_____

_____

_____

_____

_____

4. What is the difference between mere belief and real faith? We are told by the apostle Paul to test ourselves to see whether we be of the faith. How might we do this?

_____

_____

_____

_____

_____

5. There are three interconnected Sabbaths in the Bible – creation, Mosaic Law and the soul Sabbath. How do we apply these practically to our lives today?

_____

_____

_____

_____

_____

6. What do you consider the heart of the soul Sabbath?

_____

_____

_____

_____

_____

7. The Word of God is the sword of the Spirit, which we are instructed to wield. How may we do so in the world of our everyday working lives?

_____

_____

_____

_____

_____

8. Jesus has been tempted in every way just like us. Itemise some of the temptations that He must have faced and discuss how He is able to help us overcome our temptations.

_____

_____

_____

_____

_____

Personal Application

Debates about the security of our salvation are largely academic. Ask instead, 'Am I walking by faith today?' If so, you can feel sure of your security in the love of God. If not, you are warned to repent of the error of your ways. It's as simple as that.

Sometimes circumstances, doubts, fears and the welter of voices confuse us. We need the clear, unequivocal voice of God. The sword of the Spirit is the sharpest blade on earth, able to separate the very essence of our being into its constituent parts. It exposes hypocrisy and double-dealing, but equally uncovers the sincere heart that loves God. Let us examine our hearts to ensure that we rest in the grace of Christ every day, until we come to the eternal today where there are no yesterdays nor tomorrows.

Seeing Jesus in the Scriptures

Hebrews encourages us to continue steadfastly in our faith. Jesus has preceded us and speaks on our behalf. Although He is our exalted and glorious High Priest, He also understands our human condition. He has lived here and has faced the same temptations as we do. Yet He never sinned and that qualifies Him to represent us before heaven's throne of judgment.

Hard times tempt us to cynicism, to questioning the goodness of God. Even prayer seems pointless. The priesthood of Jesus assures us that heaven's throne is not an alien environment but a place of mercy and help. Our Friend and Brother is already there on our behalf and He simply wants us to join Him.

WEEK 3

Surpassing Aaron

Opening Icebreaker

This is an opportunity to make an identikit high priest.
Either put together between you characteristics you think
would make a high priest, or get each member to sponsor
a suitable characteristic they see in another member of the
group. You can do this verbally or on paper.

Bible Readings

- Hebrews 5:1–6:20
- Ephesians 4:11–16
- 1 Corinthians 3:1–4
- Luke 22:39–46

Key verse: 'You are a priest for ever, in the order
of Melchizedek.' (Heb. 5:6)

Focus: Grow up; don't give up!

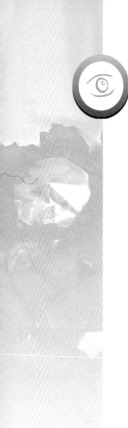

Opening Our Eyes

The high priest's task is to represent lesser mortals before the awesomeness of God. It involves offering thanks for blessings received, and offering sacrifices to atone for wrongdoings. The high priest stands in the gap; he is the mediator, monitoring the flow of divine power and expressing representatively the worship of the faithful. Yet, he himself is fragile, like those on whose behalf he acts. He must offer sacrifices for his own sins before approaching the Holy of Holies to stand before God Himself. Because the high priest understands weakness, his position is one of humility and pastoral concern for those he represents.

Fulfilling such a role is a calling. Aaron was first in a long line chosen to represent the Israelites. There is also another; Jesus is chosen by God and appointed head of a priestly order that is superior to the Aaronic order. He, too, shares the necessary vulnerability and identification with sinners. The prayer life of Jesus, culminating in Gethsemane, where Jesus felt the full horror of a human facing terrible death, makes this plain. Jesus is no stained-glass Saviour; He did not shortcut the reality of His priesthood with mere lip service to the Father's will. Jesus truly learned by doing; His painful journey to the perfection and completion of God's will for His life was utterly authentic and makes Him the true source of eternal salvation for everyone who calls Him Lord.

To consider the priesthood of Jesus is immensely profitable, but for one problem – the readers are locked into immaturity. When by now they should be teachers, they are like babies clinging to their mothers' breasts, they are as children still learning their ABC. Solid food awaits, but they must submit themselves to the discipline of training if they are to enjoy it. That training teaches us to discern good from evil – to become wise.

God wants us to grow up – Ephesians 4:11–16. We should not be rerunning the basics of Christian conversion week after week to check whether we had got it right or that we even wanted it. We cannot jump in and out of our faith at will, like children unable to make up their minds. The boat is leaving the harbour and we need to be on board. If you jump off once it is underway, there is no way that you can climb back on. All that can be said is that you jumped off and you are left behind in the water. The lesson is simple: don't do it!

To play around like is this is tantamount to crucifying Jesus all over again. It is like saying, 'He died for me and I believe, but I changed by mind. But now I'll give it another go, so He had better die for me again, hadn't He?' What arrogance! God calls us to a fruitful life; if we produce weeds then we face the danger of being cursed and torched.

This salutary caution is intended to realign a distorted perspective so that we keep on course. Indeed, despite the difficulties, these believers are bearing a good testimony, particularly by their care for others. There really is no cause to give up now. Indeed, God will keep us. He has sworn an oath and done so in His own powerful name. No way will God let us down. We hope in Him and that hope is a secure anchor for our souls.

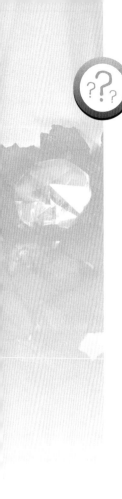

Discussion Starters

1. Discuss why you think people need priests and gurus.

_____

_____

_____

_____

2. Jesus never sinned, yet He needed to be perfected. What does this mean and what does it mean for us to be perfected?

_____

_____

_____

_____

3. What do you think keeps us locked into spiritual immaturity?

_____

_____

_____

_____

4. How do we train ourselves to distinguish good from evil? Why is this so necessary?

_____

_____

_____

_____

5. The cult of youth dominates our age and 'dumbing down' is glorified as 'cool'. What then are the virtues of maturity and old age?

_____

_____

_____

_____

6. There is a difference between someone who is fickle about their faith and one who through force of circumstances gives up in despair. How do we pastorally distinguish the two, warning of judgment for the former and offering the latter encouragement?

_____

_____

_____

_____

7. We are reminded of the parable of the sower and the way that thorns and thistles choke the seed of the Word. How can we keep our hearts as good soil?

_____

_____

_____

8. Everyone needs examples to emulate. Talk about some of the people who have inspired you to persevere.

_____

_____

_____

9. Hope is vital to our future, both for this life and the next. In what ways does hope anchor our souls?

_____

_____

_____

Personal Application

Establishing foundations shouldn't take us too long! Once laid, they should be built upon. Check that the following basics for future growth are laid in your life.

- You have repented of all known sins and self-justification.
- You have put your faith unequivocally in the God and Father of our Lord Jesus Christ.
- You have been baptised in water to acknowledge your new life.
- You have been filled with the Holy Spirit.
- You have made preparation for your resurrection from the dead at the return of Christ.
- You have put your life under the government of God.

Once done, don't grow away from these truths any more than a house ignores its foundations and plonks itself down somewhere else. Instead, grow up in these truths. If you lack in any of these areas, you should seek appropriate counsel and prayer.

Seeing Jesus in the Scriptures

It is no easy task to portray the life of Christ on film, yet the best efforts do succeed in presenting us with the wonderful mystery of God incarnate set in a believably real world.

The Christ of the Gospels laid aside His eternal attributes and became as us. All His mighty works were done in dependence on the Holy Spirit. He understands vulner-ability: born to a peasant girl, growing up among a subject people, learning a trade, facing the temptations of youth and the privations of sacrifice, submitting to death at the hands of pagans. This Jesus knows our lot in life, and He is more than willing to lend us a helping hand in our struggles.

WEEK 4

New Priesthood, New Covenant

Opening Icebreaker

What's in a name? Ask members of the group to explain the meaning of their names, first or second, and whether in any sense it describes what they are like.

Bible Readings

- Hebrews 7:1–8:13
- Genesis 14:18–20
- Psalm 110:4
- 1 Peter 2:9–10

Key verse: 'I will make a new covenant ...' (Heb. 8:8)

Focus: Jesus is the guarantee of a better covenant

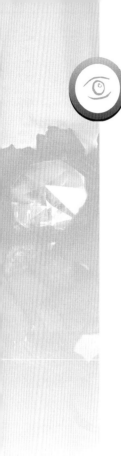

Opening Our Eyes

Mention Melchizedek and most people look blank. Few recall a small incident in Genesis 14 where Abram meets a man named Melchizedek – the king of Salem and priest of God Most High. He blesses Abram in the Creator's name and gives him bread and wine. Abram donates 10 per cent of his spoils to Melchizedek. This apparently obscure event proves incredibly significant. The Messianic Psalm 110 proclaims the coming One as a priest for ever after the order of Melchizedek. This statement is destined to render redundant an entire nationalistic priestly system and to launch a new global faith.

Melchizedek (king of righteousness – *Melech* + *tsidkenu* – and king of Salem or peace – akin to *shalom*) is the prototype representation of God's Son. Introduced without reference to his ancestry, his priesthood isn't traced by chronological descent but is timeless. The quality of the man predominates over the integrity of his ancestry. Melchizedek is greater than Abram, because Abram tithed to him, representatively tithing for all his descendants, notably Levi. This makes the Levitical priesthood subservient to that of Melchizedek. Abram, by faith anticipating in Melchizedek's priesthood the future coming of Christ, in effect tithed to Christ, and so did Levi. Melchizedek, being the greater, blessed Abram.

All this challenges the permanency of the Levitical priesthood. If it were meant to continue for ever, why did God proclaim a new priestly order for His Messiah? Jesus came not from Levi's tribe but Judah's, so He couldn't be an ancestrally determined priest, He is a Melchizedek priest, determined by the power of eternal life. Unlike Levitical priesthood, God pledged in His Son a superior order and guaranteed a better covenant.

The original covenant proved ineffective because the law cannot reconcile people to God. We need a fresh start, a new priestly order, and Jesus provides precisely that. Whereas Levitical priests died, Jesus is permanently installed so that all people through all ages may benefit from His intercession. Unlike the Levites, Jesus has no need to make daily sacrifices for His sins. Instead He offered Himself for our sins once and for all and is now seated at the right hand of God, serving in the heavenly tabernacle.

This tabernacle is the spiritual reality upon which the earthly copy was modelled – and that's why Moses had to follow so closely the architectural plans for the tabernacle given by God. Clearly the reality is better than the copy, so when we worship today we do not focus on earthly buildings and rituals. Instead, 'A time is coming and has now come when the true worshippers will worship the Father in spirit and truth' (John 4:23). This better priestly order and the true tabernacle herald a new, better covenant that provides the basis for the entire Christian faith. The first covenant failed through the unfaithfulness of people and served only to demonstrate the sinfulness of human nature. The new one is different:

• Instead of the law being on tablets of stone, it will be written on our hearts.
• Instead of our being exiled and abandoned as in the past, He will be unshakeably and unashamedly God to His people, and we will be faithful in return.
• Instead of constant appeals to know the Lord personally, we shall all know Him, irrespective of our status.
• Instead of being constantly judged for our sins, they will be totally obliterated.

This wonderful new covenant renders the old obsolete and destined imminently to disappear.

Discussion Starters

1. In what ways does the Melchizedek incident challenge western ways of thinking?

_____

_____

_____

_____

2. Abraham had a new covenant faith even before the old covenant had been given. The fact that he tithed provides a basis for us who stand in his faith also to tithe to Christ. What do you think?

_____

_____

_____

_____

3. What do you consider to be the contrast between the Levitical priesthood and the Melchizedek priesthood?

_____

_____

_____

_____

4. What comfort can we draw from the fact that Jesus is always interceding for us?

_____

_____

_____

_____

5. What do you understand by the heavenly tabernacle? There are clues in Revelation 4–8.

_____

_____

_____

_____

6. Why has God declared the Jewish sacrificial system redundant? What do we have to offer Jews today?

_____

_____

_____

_____

7. Discuss what it means for God's law to be written on our hearts. Give examples of how this operates.

_____

_____

_____

_____

8. We are described as a royal priesthood. This is in the order of Jesus our great High Priest. How do we exercise our ministry of the new covenant?

_____

_____

_____

_____

9. What is the significance of Melchizedek giving Abraham bread and wine?

_____

_____

_____

_____

Personal Application

If Jesus were not a High Priest of the order of Melchizedek, we would have no certainty of salvation. Indeed, we would still be performing animal sacrifices and looking to an unbroken succession of earthly priests to represent us. As it is, we can have complete security in the effectiveness of His sacrifice on the cross for our sins and in the permanency of His intercession on our behalf.

When we feel tempted to despair because of our poor performance, we should fix our eyes on the power and effectiveness of our High Priest. Jesus never fails to meet the needs of those who put their trust in Him. When New Age people talk about their occult masters, gurus and shamans, we should have every confidence to speak about the virtues of Jesus – He outshines the lot and has rendered all the rest redundant!

Seeing Jesus in the Scriptures

Consider the qualifications of Jesus to this highest office.

- He stands in a timeless line.
- He is tithed to by the father of the faithful.
- He bestows blessings on His people.
- He is sworn in by God Himself.
- He lives for ever and prays unceasingly.
- He is holy, blameless and pure.
- He offered His own self for our transgressions.
- He is at the right hand of God.
- He serves the true tabernacle.
- He ministers the new covenant that writes God's law on our hearts, makes us His special people, brings us into a personal relationship with Him, and forgives all our sins.

WEEK 5

Entering the True Tabernacle

Opening Icebreaker

If you wanted to make a house for God to meet you under the old covenant, what essential features would you give it? What would the house look like if you built it for Jesus to meet you under the new covenant?

Bible Readings

- Hebrews 9:1–10:18
- Isaiah 53:4–11
- Colossians 2:13–17

Key verse: 'How much more, then, will the blood of Christ … cleanse our consciences …' (Heb. 9:14)

Focus: The blood of Christ is the final and perfect offering for our sins

Opening Our Eyes

One very good reason for reading the Old Testament is to make sense of the New. Take the worship structure of the earthly tabernacle that Moses erected in the wilderness. What is the significance of the items, their layout, the priests, and the once-a-year entrance of the high priest into the Holy of Holies?

It all pointed to a time when the Holy Spirit would open the way for all peoples to approach God all of the time. The entire elaborate system provided an external paradigm to pave the way for the arrival of the new order. Of itself it was powerless to ease the consciences of the devout, let alone erase the sins of the vast peoples that constituted the Gentile world.

All that has changed. Look now at the true heavenly tabernacle where Jesus has entered on our behalf. Travel beyond the externals of the crucifixion and gain an insight into the deeper passion of the Christ. Those terrible physical sufferings of Jesus, hinting as they do at His awful spiritual anguish, are the ultimate sin offering for the world. Animal sacrifices may have granted some external, technical, ceremonial status of cleansing, but they could never cleanse the heart. At best they provided an alternative to that tendency of people to offer human sacrifices. However, the Lamb of God, a perfect sacrifice and human like us, truly cleanses our consciences to serve the living God. This is the new covenant mediated to us by Jesus. Transcending time, it reaches back to cleanse the faithful who sinned under the old covenant and forwards to embrace us.

Why the emphasis upon shed blood, particularly in an age when we prefer to see religion as a matter of enlightenment rather than of redemption? Blood represents life and its shedding, death. These prefiguring sacrifices of the old covenant indicated a death – the sacrifice of the Lamb of God (Isa. 53). The new covenant was a promised inheritance; however, an inheritance is only realised upon the proven death of the benefactor. Well, Jesus has died, not in the man-made tabernacle, but in the true heavenly one.

Jesus needed to make His offering only the once; no repeat sacrifices are needed. The next visit of Christ to this earth will be as the King of Glory to effect the final redemption of those who await His return.

The abolition of an entire religious system is a big claim to make. Yet consider the matter: if the Old Testament sacrifices were efficacious they would need no repetition. That very repetition is a proof of their inadequacy. The blood of animals cannot remove sin.

There was needed someone who would fulfil the conditions – a Son long prophesied, sent from God not in ritualistic obedience but as a servant who would use His God-given body to glorify His Father in willing self-sacrifice. This being done by Jesus, once and for all, has made us acceptable to God.

The earthly priest's work is never done. However futile his offerings, he must keep on making them. Christ, however, has sat down at the right hand of God. His work is finished. That is the significance of His cry on the cross. It is accomplished. Christ the Victor now waits until His enemies become His footstool. The great new covenant promises are inaugurated. The law is now internalised and our sins are forgotten. There need be no more offerings for sin. Christ has suffered enough.

Discussion Starters

1. Religion is a worldwide phenomenon. Why do people need religion and why is the new covenant really a religionless religion?

_____

_____

_____

_____

2. A sense of guilt and a need for justice and atonement lie at the heart of the Old Testament ceremonial system. How do we make the connection between these truths and the reality of our neighbours' lives?

_____

_____

_____

_____

3. External rituals cannot change us. Read Romans 14:17 and Colossians 2:20–23. How does Jesus replace our obsession with dietary rules and bodily disciplines?

_____

_____

_____

_____

4. If the earthly tabernacle was a copy of the heavenly, and if we are the temple of the Holy Spirit, what should be the heavenly characteristics of our lives?

_____

_____

_____

_____

5. People today object to the idea of blood sacrifice. Can we really have a cross-less Christianity? Why is the blood of Christ so important?

_____

_____

_____

_____

_____

6. Jesus died once and for all. In so doing He rendered all religious sacrifices redundant. How would you share this truth with those of other faiths?

_____

_____

_____

_____

_____

7. How will the enemies of Jesus become His footstool? What does this mean?

_____

_____

_____

_____

_____

8. We struggle with the word 'sin' today, yet 1 John 1:8–10 tells us that the acknowledgment of our sinfulness is non-negotiable if we want to know God. How do we convince people that they are sinners?

_____

_____

_____

_____

_____

Personal Application

Good parents develop a bad memory for their children's misdemeanours once matters have been dealt with. In this they reflect God's heart. Jesus having paid the price for our sins, God chooses to forget all our wrongdoing. We need not keep coming to God with the wretched burden of a lifetime's worth of sin. Instead, He invites us to approach the throne of grace with the confidence of children who trust their Father's love. We still have daily faults to confess – that is part of growing up – but our status is no longer that of sinners. We are all sons and daughters of God through faith in Christ Jesus.

What an inspiration to live! What self-worth it gives us! Sinning always takes away self-respect. By choosing righteousness we affirm our new status in Christ and we honour His sacrifice on our behalf.

Seeing Jesus in the Scriptures

John the Baptist pointed to Jesus and said, 'Behold the Lamb of God who takes away the sin of the world.' It was a radical, prophetic statement. Jesus was the fulfilment of Isaiah 53, dealing with sin and rendering all other offerings obsolete, not just for the Jews but for the entire world.

The magnitude of this is staggering. Christ bore the wickedness, perversity, fallibility, destructiveness and sheer self-centredness of every single person on earth. He opened the way for all who come with a penitent heart, irrespective of their creed, race, gender, status, age or education. Read John 3:16 and remember with gratitude that it includes you.

WEEK 6

Keep the Faith

Opening Icebreaker

Each member of the group chooses a favourite Bible hero (other than Jesus) and explains why and how that character inspires his or her life today.

Bible Readings

- Hebrews 10:19–12:3
- Genesis 15:1–6
- 1 Corinthians 10:10–13

Key verse: 'Now faith is being sure of what we hope for and certain of what we do not see.' (Heb. 11:1)

Focus: It is really worth persevering in our faith

Opening Our Eyes

Persevere, you saints! Faith has triumphant power. Christ is your High Priest, Sacrifice and the Mediator of a better covenant, so approach God with confidence. The Holy of Holies is open for you to enter the intimate presence of God. Seize this reality and stir one another to acts of loving service. Some have stopped meeting together, but they are wrong. We should gather regularly to encourage one another, particularly in the light of Christ's return.

Temptations to abandon the faith are real, but they make us face an uncomfortable logic. If we reject God's salvation in Christ and return to Jewish rituals, let alone paganism, we put ourselves beyond God's help. There is no alternative to Jesus; no other offering for sin; nothing else but impending judgment. The Mosaic Law had inbuilt judgments, even more so does the new covenant.

This refers to more than backsliding because of a sense of failure or discouragement. It is the wilful rejection of the faith, which is to profane the cross of Christ, to ridicule His shed blood and to reject the kindness and mercy of God's Holy Spirit. People who do that put themselves beyond the pale and face a terrifying judgment.

These stern words are meant to caution us, but not to raise uncertainties about our salvation. They invite us to ask whether we really want to contemplate apostasy. Having travelled so far despite persecution and privation wherein they had shown courage and loyalty to one another, these people had proved the reality of their faith. They had laughed when their persecutors stole their earthly possessions because they could live by invisible means and in anticipation of a heavenly city. Quite right, too! God would vindicate them. Christ will come again. Giving up isn't their style.

We stand in a long and noble line of people whose faith is in a Creator God. Remember Abel who understood the need for blood sacrifice even though it cost him his own life; Enoch, who walked so close to God that he was transmuted straight into glory; Noah, who built the ark and preached righteousness despite the wickedness around him.

Abraham set out into the unknown with his eyes of faith set on a heavenly city. By faith he sired a nation when humanly it seemed impossible. Offering his son Isaac, he discovered substitutionary atonement and resurrection.

Isaac himself blessed the family line and Joseph blessed his 12 sons, even prophesying the Exodus. Moses' parents hid him, and Moses himself chose dishonour for the sake of Christ rather than the glamour of Egypt. He inaugurated the Passover and led the people across the Red Sea towards the promised land.

Years passed, but God is faithful and Jericho fell. Rahab believed, leaving her paganism and prostitution behind. What of the judges and prophets – and all those noble martyrs whose worth shames the world? Did they die in vain? No, all these people acted in faith even though they never saw the promises fulfilled.

That awaited us heirs of the new covenant. Intimately linked with the heroes of the past we run our marathon surrounded by their encouraging presence. Above all, there is Jesus, the origin and the goal of our faith – the greatest hero of all and the mightiest man of faith. Jesus chose to despise the ignominy and to endure the sufferings. Now He is in the place of supreme honour. Surely, we have no cause to give up!

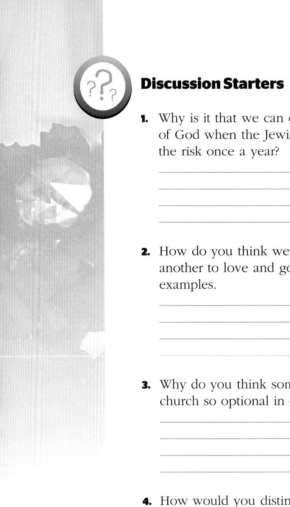

Discussion Starters

1. Why is it that we can come so easily into the presence of God when the Jewish high priest could only take the risk once a year?

_____

_____

_____

_____

2. How do you think we can practically spur one another to love and good works? Come up with some examples.

_____

_____

_____

_____

3. Why do you think some Christians find attending church so optional in our current climate?

_____

_____

_____

_____

4. How would you distinguish between the discouraged backslider and the wilful apostate?

_____

_____

_____

_____

5. 'The fear of the Lord is the beginning of wisdom.' What has this passage in Hebrews to teach us about the awesomeness of God?

_____

_____

_____

_____

6. People sometimes confuse faith with hope. What is the difference and how do you recognise it?

_____

_____

_____

_____

7. How would you describe the heavenly city that the heroes of faith sought for?

_____

_____

_____

_____

8. What are the sins and encumbrances that most commonly hinder us running the race?

_____

_____

_____

_____

9. By what practical means can we consider Christ so that we do not grow weary in our faith?

_____

_____

_____

_____

Personal Application

It's easy to lose our perspective, to become overwhelmed with our immediate difficulties. Is it all worth it? At such times we need the inspiration of history. Our lives form part of a great movement spanning the ages and, despite faults and failings, we may be proud of our heritage. Nor should we despise our own journey. We paid a price to follow Jesus; it is worth it, for the present and the future.

Trials are common to humanity, yet God always provides a way for us to cope, often through mutual encouragement. When many of God's people consider attending church highly optional, we must remind ourselves of our responsibilities to one another. It is less what we get out of church, but more what we give to encourage others.

Seeing Jesus in the Scriptures

Our greatest inspiration is Jesus Himself. Raised with a question mark over His parentage, tempted by Satan, misunderstood by His peers, threatened by the authorities, betrayed by His friends, He endured the entire road to Calvary.

Jesus was no passive victim. He had the power at any time to opt out. The brutal scourging alone might have killed Him. The dreadful procession to Golgotha could have terminated His life. Despite the sheer pain, He pressed on until He, beyond our comprehension, became sin for us – until He could cry triumphantly, 'It is accomplished'. We need to fix our eyes continuously upon Him. Surely, we cannot despise His self-sacrifice, nor fail to honour the spirit of grace that has touched our lives.

WEEK 7

Towards Maturity

Opening Icebreaker

Share testimonies of hard experiences in your lives that have produced character, strength and maturity.

Bible Readings

- Hebrews 12:4–13:25
- 2 Corinthians 4:7–18
- Romans 8:18–21

Key verse: 'Endure hardship as discipline; God is treating you as sons.' (Heb. 12:7)

Focus: God lovingly coaches us to maturity by means of our tough times

Opening Our Eyes

This final section exhorts us to persevere and succeed in our faith. The sufferings of Jesus and the testimony of the heroes of the faith remind us that sometimes we need a restored sense of proportion, if only to realise that there's always someone worse off than ourselves. Most of our pity parties are unjustified.

A loving purpose is at work in our hardships. Because we are sons and daughters of God, He disciplines us through our circumstances so that we will grow up strong and healthy. This is not punishment, but correction and training. All decent earthly parents recognise the need to train their children to behave well and make wise choices. It doesn't come naturally. Children are inherently selfish and wilful so the process is often uncomfortable for both parent and child. However, later, adults will respect their parents for the discipline. How much more so our heavenly Father! Our earthly parents made mistakes, but our heavenly Father gets it right every time. However discomforting the process, the end result is goodness and peace.

So, don't surrender to self-pity! Co-operate with the process by strengthening your spiritual sinews and choosing God's paths. Wander off in a weakened state and you may become completely disabled and miss God's wholesome purpose. Instead, apply yourself to the two great commands: love God and love your neighbours. This is the heart of true holiness. Take responsibility together to prevent bitterness taking root in your hearts. Cynicism is a pernicious weed that poisons lives. Esau lost his inheritance through momentary folly and despite his tears never regained it. Succumbing to sexual temptation, in particular, can wreck lives.

This vulnerability occurs when we misinterpret God's parental discipline as judicial punishment. It is a choice of mountains – Sinai or Zion. We have not come to Sinai with its terrifying judgments, but to the heavenly city full of joyful angels and God's redeemed people. Jesus and all His children are there because of a sacrifice even greater than Abel's first offering.

Don't become petulant, bitter or self-destructive. How foolish to refuse God's love and return to a fleetingly attractive world under judgment. God plans to shake the entire cosmos so that only His kingdom will remain stable. Instead of bemoaning our fate, let's be grateful and worship God with due reverence, for He is a consuming fire.

Enough of this self-pity then! Love one another, entertain strangers – who might just be angels. Care for those who suffer, especially prisoners for the faith. Resist the surrounding immorality, respect marriage and do not commit adultery. Don't be obsessed with acquiring earthly wealth, since God supplies all your needs. Honour your leaders and respect their authority. They care for your souls before God, so don't make their task any harder by stubborn rebellion.

Avoid wacky doctrines of self-salvation. Special diets will not save souls; real nourishment is found at the heavenly altar. It may mean accepting dishonour for Christ, but better a fool for Him than a fool for the devil. Jesus was executed outside the city as unclean to procure our sanctification. Don't be ashamed to join Him, pilgrims, your eyes look for a *new* Jerusalem!

Our lives then should be characterised by worship, kindness and prayer for the faithful. Let us pray that the God of peace and pastoral love will equip us to fulfil God's will. Receive this exhortation with a good heart and grow in the grace of the Lord.

Discussion Starters

1. What is the place of discipline in raising children? How do we learn from the way that God disciplines us?

_____

_____

_____

_____

2. Give some suggestions as to how we strengthen our weak arms and knees and make straight paths for our feet.

_____

_____

_____

_____

3. How do we identify and deal with the roots of bitterness?

_____

_____

_____

_____

4. What are the contrasts between Mount Sinai and Mount Zion? How do these affect our outlook on life?

_____

_____

_____

_____

5. What do you think it means when God says He will shake the earth and the heavens?

_____

_____

_____

_____

6. Why is hospitality so highly regarded in the Bible?

7. Money, sex and power remain three major areas of temptation. What can we do together to avoid succumbing to them?

8. This is an age of self-improvement techniques, diets, etc. How do you explain to a New Ager your source of inner nourishment?

9. What does it mean to join Jesus 'outside the camp' and yet still be intimately involved with the life of society?

10. What are the conditions upon which we are to obey our spiritual leaders?

Personal Application

This section concludes the author's intent to encourage, challenge and strengthen those who are wavering in their faith. Biblical admonition is robust; it doesn't pander to our self-pity. Rather it appeals to our true calling. We are sons and daughters of God and our Father is coaching us so that we reach maturity. Inevitably, we go through tough times, but the end result is healthy strength. We are being trained for a place among the elect company of the redeemed.

It is a good practice to perform a life review occasionally and to examine our present trials in the light of God's training purpose. We may be surprised at how far we have travelled. There is a warning here, too: if we drop out, we forfeit the possibility of spiritual growth and maturity. So don't give up!

Seeing Jesus in the Scriptures

Jesus is the one constant in our lives, unchanging in character, faithfulness and love. We can rely totally upon Him. God calls us to identify with Him and His cause, even if that means sharing in His public dishonour. He willingly became unclean for us, knowing that God would vindicate Him. God honoured the eternal covenant made between Him and His Son and He raised Jesus from the dead. The Good Shepherd who laid down His life for His flock is alive and well and with us.

God who so loved His Son also loves us and He will both vindicate us and provide everything we need to fulfil His will in our own lives.

Leader's Notes

Week 1: Brighter than Angels

Open this first session by reading the Introduction, but do not allow much discussion over the authorship of Hebrews since that is not the purpose of the meeting.

Opening Icebreaker

The Icebreaker is designed to get people speaking about their spiritual experiences and their sense of a spiritual world. Remind people that most of the activity of angels is invisible to our eyes.

Aim of the Session

Share out the readings, but if time is tight simply concentrate on the section from Hebrews, encouraging people to read the others at their leisure.

The opening chapters reveal the writer's intention to establish Jesus as the greatest spiritual authority in the universe. He begins with the world of supernatural beings, with God Himself and with angels, but sets Jesus above the angels as the proper object of our worship. Do emphasise that Jesus is the Message and not simply the communicator of the Message. God's answer to the world isn't another sermon, code of conduct or list of rules – it is His own Son.

Try not to become bogged down in Trinitarian discussions about the relationship of the Son to the Father. It is enough to say that this passage teaches that the Son is coequal with the Father in nature, in activity and in glory.

The eternal Son became one of us; He walked our world and identified with our pains to the point of laying down

His life for us. Jesus defeated the devil on our behalf and made atonement for our sins. He even calls us His family.

These words are addressed to believers struggling to maintain their faith in a hostile environment. Rather than urging us to stoicism, or to a happy sing-sing in a holy huddle, the writer focuses on the weightiness of our calling. The Son of God Himself has spoken to us and destined us to salvation – authoritatively but also compassionately, for He understands our problems and shares our journey.

Try to avoid futile arguments about the security or otherwise of our salvation based upon Hebrews 2:2–3. The point here is simply that there is only one way of salvation. Because there are no other alternatives it would be stupid to turn away from it.

When using the Discussion Starters, you should refer people to the text where appropriate. The second reminds us that we must challenge people with more than a belief in God. Jesus said, 'You believe in God, believe also in me'. This is fundamental to salvation: to be saved we must confess that Jesus Christ is Lord and believe that God has raised Him from the dead. Encourage the group to reaffirm the divinity of Jesus vocally and together in the words of Peter: 'I believe that you are the Christ, the Son of the living God.' Discussion Starter 8 may raise some pastoral issues regarding the fear of death. Many people say they are not afraid of dying, provided it is painless, but the fear of death is common to the human race and manifested in greed, oppression and arrogance as well as depression and apathy. Find a suitable counselling context for any who are experiencing times of doubt and fear.

The Personal Application reminds us of the myth of value-free education and society. We all believe something that we have heard, whether fully conscious of that fact or not. It is better to heed the call of heaven than the blare of hell.

If time permits, read Revelation 1:12–16 and conclude with an opportunity to worship the glorified Lord Jesus Christ.

Week 2: Greater than Moses

Opening Icebreaker
The purpose of this is both to help us learn a bit more about one another and to remind us of the importance of rest and relaxation in the light of the Sabbath principle that runs throughout Scripture.

Aim of the Session
We are invited to consider two spheres of apostolic authority by comparing Moses and Jesus. If Moses was a great man, then Jesus is greater. The law came by Moses, but grace and truth came by Jesus Christ. Moses founded the nation of Israel and Jesus founded the worldwide household of faith.

Moses had to lead a bunch of rebels who became illustrative of those who, in spite of every encouragement, harden their hearts against the gospel and are full of unbelief. As a consequence, they lost whatever inheritance they might have gained and died in the wilderness having failed to reach God's promised rest. Their example is used by the writer to caution us against the same folly, reminding us that sitting under the sound of the gospel and agreeing with the truth is insufficient to save us. We need faith, and faith is an action word that commits our lives to walking a path and continuing until the end.

It is better not to get bogged down in Calvinist versus Arminian arguments about eternal security. That debate

has little to do with how the Bible tackles the question of perseverance. The Scriptures are pragmatic and realistic. If we are worried about our eternal fate, then we need simply to ensure that we are resting in the saving work of Christ today and when tomorrow comes to do the same again, and the next day. However, if we choose to ignore this counsel, then little assurance can be given because we are not in the place to receive such assurance.

The Word of God searches our hearts. It reveals to us the truth about ourselves. Many believers experience hard times and are beset by personal weaknesses and doubts, but nonetheless in the depths of their beings truly follow Christ and have faith in His saving work at Calvary. Such people simply need reminding of who Jesus is, how much He loves them, and how He understands fully their weaknesses and is still prepared to represent them before the throne of heaven. This itself encourages people both to continue in the faith and slowly to overcome their frailties.

That same Word of God also exposes hypocrisy and the arrogance of those who perhaps find leading a disciplined, moral and religious life comes naturally to them. Such people may actually be quite hardened in their hearts and they need to enter God's rest where they cease from self-righteousness and trust in Jesus.

The Discussion Starters allow us to explore these matters interactively. The true spiritual life is one characterised by an inner rest based upon complete trust in Christ. This should condition the way that we live and the degree to which we, in our frenetic work-driven consumerist society, take time to Sabbath. You may wish to have some constructive debate on how we might obey the Sabbath commandment in our present world.

Jesus was tempted in the wilderness with the only three possible sins – the lust of the flesh, the lust of the eyes and the pride of life. These He overcame by the Word of God. Other temptations confronted Him in His life, but they were all out-workings of the three great sins. Help people to see that their situations are not unique. You may find it helpful to read out 1 Corinthians 10:13.

Week 3: Surpassing Aaron

Aim of the Session

This section completes the triple superiority of Christ by establishing Him as the great High Priest. The implications of this priesthood will be worked out in the next session. The journey has taken us from the eternal world of the angels, through the wilderness experience, to the establishment of a form of worship that was to last almost uninterrupted until AD 70. It is no light thing to propose a new high priest and, therefore, a new form of worship, but that is exactly what the writer does. Jesus is fully qualified by virtue of God's appointing and by virtue of His true humanity. You should remind people of the Gospels and of the pen portraits they paint of our Saviour.

Having established that Jesus is our new High Priest, the writer switches to a pastoral concern. It is an all too common one today, particularly in churches that lack a good disciple-ship process and teaching ministry. Too many Christians are reprehensibly ignorant of the Scriptures and immature in their behaviour. We feel like crying, 'Why don't you grow up!' Believers need to sort out their foundations once and for all and get on with the task of living and maturing.

This brings us to one of the difficult passages in Scripture. Traditionally, people have argued from doctrinal positions that believe either that salvation is utterly predestined and secure or that it can be lost by our wilfulness. This displays a mindset that believes truth can be enshrined

in a static proposition, but truth is dynamic and is connected to the activity of life rather than to theological speculations. The writer wants us to realise the incongruity of having had so much that is so good, then playing the fool with it. It is outrageous to treat the death of Christ and its command over our lives as something to be picked up and put down at will. So the emphasis in our meeting should not be upon the old debate, but rather on an appeal to the heart. Can we really turn back in the light of all that God has given to us? Can we really trample the blood of Jesus underfoot simply because we are finding life difficult? Can we take lives offered to God for spiritual fruitfulness and donate them to the cultivation of weeds?

This passage is not meant to threaten people or to cause doubts where there need be none. It is meant to encourage us on our path. The writer identifies the good that these people have accomplished and assures them that it is worth sticking with it. For our salvation is underwritten by God Himself and He has sworn an oath that we would inherit the promises. So you should concentrate on the hope that is set before us, which is like an anchor for our souls in stormy weather.

Try to keep the discussion to major issues and focus on the importance of growing up, bearing good fruit and reaching spiritual maturity.

When you come to the Personal Application, it may be good to open up the discussion to allow people to say honestly where they are in their Christian lives. Depending upon the nature of your group, you may offer counsel there and then, or arrange private sessions.

The section Seeing Jesus will be an opportunity for people to talk about films they have seen of the life of Christ and it may be good for the group to arrange at some point to hire a copy for viewing together.

Week 4: New Priesthood, New Covenant

Opening Icebreaker

This provides an opportunity for us to think about the meaning of names and their effect on character in cultures other than ours.

Aim of the Session

Don't be put off by the apparent complexity of the writer's argument. This is an incredibly important part of Scripture, defining as it does the entire basis for our Christian faith and why we are not still seeking rightness with God through blood-sacrifices. It will be good to read the little incident in Genesis 14 and then to explain the meaning of Melchizedek's name.

When you come to describe the way that Abraham tithed to Melchizedek it may help to draw a little picture. Draw Abraham and inside him, draw Levi. Draw Melchizedek and behind him, larger and in dotted lines, draw Jesus. Abraham tithes to Melchizedek, but is in faith tithing to Christ. The yet unconceived Levi is committed to tithing likewise to Melchizedek/Jesus.

The fact that the new covenant replaces the pre-AD 70 sacrificial system of the Jews should not be taken as anti-Semitic and we may continue to respect contemporary Jewish religion and culture. Where we have opportunity, we should invite Jews to reconsider the claims of Jesus to be their Messiah.

One way of considering this passage is as the legal contract and basis for our faith. It is underwritten and signed by God Himself. The point of this is to give us absolute security in the gospel and in the validity of Jesus as the Son of God and our great High Priest. This is important in days when Jesus, though respected for His humanity, is often denied His deity. People still need to confess with Peter,

'You are the Christ, the Son of the Living God'. When you deal with the four main items of the new covenant, try to apply these in a devotional manner to the lives of those present. It would be good to check out that each member of your group has entered into the fullness of each part of the covenant.

The Discussion Starters invite us to reflect upon the passage. The first one is intended to help us see that there are other ways of thinking. Logically, we would say that Melchizedek must have had parents, but the biblical way of thinking invites us not to look at the hidden background, but to consider a cameo portrait and to use that as a gateway into the deeper revelation of God. The second raises issues about Christian giving and whether we should still tithe under the new covenant. Don't spend the entire session on this!

We are often very earthbound in our thinking. Discussion Starter 5 will help us set our eyes on eternal realities when we worship. You may wish to delve into parts of Revelations 4–8 to understand this better.

Clearly if Jesus is our High Priest, then we too are priests. Irrespective of whether we feel we have a special ministry of intercession, we all have an intercessory role and you should encourage everyone to pray on behalf of those around them. The last Discussion Starter invites us to consider the Lord's Supper and, if it is appropriate in your context, then you may wish to take communion together.

The Personal Application section is to encourage us never to be ashamed of Jesus, particularly in the face of those who are claiming all manner of alternative and esoteric saviours. If you need any further encouragement, then the Seeing Jesus section gives a good number of reasons to thank God for our Saviour and High Priest.

Week 5: Entering the True Tabernacle

Opening Icebreaker

Drawing a distinction between the distancing of God under the old covenant and the nearness of God under the new can reveal much about the effect of the gospel on our perception of God.

Opening Our Eyes

The old covenant paradigm lays the groundwork for redemption, teaching us both why we need it and how it is to come about in Christ. Draw out the continual contrasts between the repetitive and ineffective sacrifices of the Old Testament system and the once-and-for-all sacrifice of Jesus. Likewise, people need to understand how the earthly tabernacle pointed to the eternal spiritual realities. The logic is very simple; if a sacrifice works it does not need repeating. The very command to repeat the sacrifices was evidence that this was just a long-term exercise pointing to the coming of Christ. Those with the eyes to see under the old covenant understood this.

The Discussion Starters invite us to look at the place of religion in the world and to recognise that if even a God-ordained religion could not save us, then certainly no other can. In a real sense the death of Christ abolished religion as a way of getting right with God. That doesn't mean we can substitute a vague spirituality or enlightenment for the Person and work of Christ. The spirit of antichrist denies that Jesus came in the flesh. Indeed an early Christian heresy addressed by the apostle John suggested that a phantom died on the cross, rather than a real, flesh-and-blood human being. The Old Testament sacrifices and the Gospel narratives combine to force us to recognise the reality of sin and judgment and the need for atonement. Discussion Starter 2 reminds us that the popular asceticism advocated in

so many magazines will never solve our inner need of reconciliation with God. Discussion Starter 7 invites us to look at Psalm 2 and the return of Christ. People and powers will serve Him willingly now, or they will cower in the face of His glory.

This message of the cross will always stumble the religious and befuddle the intellectuals. It is nonetheless the power of God to salvation to all those who believe. We should not be offensive in our manner of witness, but we cannot avoid the offence of the cross. Before any of us can be saved, we have to acknowledge humbly that we needed Jesus to suffer for us because we are guilty.

The success of Jesus' sacrifice changes our inner nature and our status. God's law is on our hearts as something now desirable and our sins are out of mind. Encourage people that the best way for Christians to avoid sinning is not to keep reminding themselves of their sinfulness, but to remind themselves of their new status as sons and daughters of God in Christ Jesus. That said, some in the group may need help with persistent sins in their lives and you should arrange private counsel for such.

You may wish to conclude this session by focusing on the generosity of God and the universal reach of Christ's sacrifice. Nobody is outside of His redemptive reach and it may be good to pray for people known to us, including those who seem impossible to save, that they too might experience the grace of God.

Week 6: Keep the Faith

Aim of the Session

This session stresses the need for perseverance in the faith, particularly for those who are struggling. Here we reach the heart of the pastoral appeal of the entire book. It contains both an encouragement and a warning – the goodness and the severity of God. Do ensure that you address both equally and keep the emphasis on the pastoral nature of the argument. This is not an academic discussion about whether we can or cannot lose our faith, it is an appeal to those who have faith to continue faithfully whatever the cost or consequences.

Some will feel insecure over the cautionary passage, fearing that because they sin they must have forfeited their salvation. Remind them that all Christians sin since we are not yet perfected, but that is far removed from a wilful choice to abandon the faith and to become violently opposed to it. The writer is deliberately forcing to their full extreme the implications of apostasy: to reject Christ is to reject God's one and only valid offer of salvation. Outside of that there is only judgment. Sombre as it is, the writer is convinced that his readers do not want to take this route. It is like asking, 'Do you really want to electrocute yourself? Surely you are not that stupid!'

Encourage people to think back on the faithfulness of God and on the battles that they have fought and won. More experienced Christians may be able to offer encouragement to the younger at this point. You might also wish to direct the group's attention to those many faithful people throughout the world today who suffer for their Christian faith. Later on in the meeting, you may wish to pray for them.

Most of this section is dedicated to the encouragement of history. We have a noble ancestry and may rightly speak

with pride of those who have shared our faith. Indeed, these people endured their hardships and trials before Christ had come. They were still in the stage of historic anticipation. We live after the coming of Christ and so it is actually easier for us to believe. Try to apply some of the experiences of these people to our contemporary experiences. It is likely that those people mentioned from verses 33 to 38 include the faithful witnesses during the time of the Maccabees around 164 BC.

The Discussion Starters are mostly self-explanatory. The first is designed to ensure that we understand the power of Christ's death and the significance of justification by faith. The third may raise some negative criticisms of the Church. This needs to be handled fairly, since some of those criticisms may be justified, but it should not be allowed to degenerate into a knock-the-leaders session. The fourth Discussion Starter may raise some anguished concerns about loved ones, particularly children, who appear to have abandoned their childhood faith. Rather than offering academic answers, we should encourage prayer for such children to experience the fullness of salvation. The answer to Discussion Starter 6 is that faith is acting now on the certainty of a future promise. The heavenly city referred to in Discussion Starter 7 is described in the language of a parallel reality in Revelation 21–22 and you may wish to refer to that.

The goal of this session is that members of the group depart with an enhanced sense of the worth of their faith and a determination to remain faithful in their generation. It may be good to end with a mutual commitment by group members to encourage one another in the race.

Week 7: Towards Maturity

Aim of the Session

This concluding section includes many exhortations to persevere in the faith. It explains to us the importance of discipline in our Christian lives. In a self-indulgent generation, some may find this a difficult concept, perhaps because they suffered a lack of personal discipline in their own upbringing. These may well find themselves interpreting their trials and temptations as a sign that God doesn't love them or that the Christian faith doesn't work, or that they are just not cut out for it. This passage helps us to understand the truth and encourages us to co-operate with the training, rather than baulk at it through self-pity. The Icebreaker will provide an opportunity for those with a better perspective to share their experiences.

This better perspective contrasts two mountains and gives us an opportunity to examine just how we view God. Is it in an old covenant manner, or a new covenant manner? You need to remind people that holy and righteous as God undoubtedly is, He is nonetheless on our side and working for our good.

The questions for discussion focus largely on how we can help one another to respond positively to God's purpose in our lives. There will always be temptations to cynicism and despair, to compromise, to the false comforts of illicit sex, consumerism and alternative spiritualities. That is part of our lot in life. However, if we will assist one another, draw on God's grace and keep our eyes on the goal, we need not succumb. As is so often the case, our outward behaviour reveals our true belief system, which may be a distorted one, because of damaged roots in our personal histories. Try to help the group members get beneath their superficial responses and examine these underlying factors. This may provoke the need for personal counsel in some.

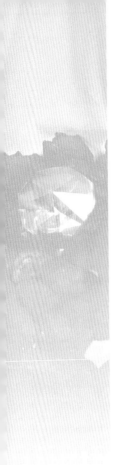

Good spiritual leadership seeks to bring people to maturity by example and instruction. It is in that context that we should obey our leaders. The command to obey leaders is not a carte blanche for leaders to usurp their authority over people's lives – yet nor are we to tolerate spiritual anarchy, for that destroys everything. We should recognise that God has appointed spheres of authority in life – the state, parents, employers, and so on. Church leaders have their sphere within this wider context of God's kingdom.

God has placed us in the world, yet He has done so as strangers and pilgrims. Discussion Starter 9 invites us to explore how we live with being in the world, but not of it. You should try to draw out very practical examples from the lives of the group members.

So much of this book is about obtaining a renewed perspective on life and you may wish to encourage people to undertake a personal life review with a trusted counsellor. This may bring about some lifestyle changes, but more likely all that is needed is a refreshed outlook. It will be good to read together the benediction from Hebrews 13:20–21 and then to pray for one another. Members of the group may wish also to reaffirm their commitment to help one another in their spiritual journeys. Above all, you need to remind people to keep their eyes fixed on Jesus, the Author and the Finisher of our faith, who is the same yesterday, today and for ever.

Notes...

Be inspired by God.
Every day.

Cover to Cover | EVERY **DAY** JAN/FEB 2017

One-year subscriptions available for all titles

Genesis 12–50
John 12–21

Bringing you deeper biblical understanding | CWR

Cover to Cover Every Day

In-depth study of the Bible, book by book. Part of a five-year series. Available as an email subscription or on eBook and Kindle.

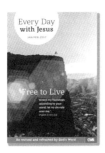

Every Day with Jesus

The popular daily Bible reading notes by Selwyn Hughes.

Inspiring Women Every Day

Daily insight and encouragement written by women for women.

Life Every Day

Lively Bible notes, with Jeff Lucas' wit and wisdom.

To order or subscribe, visit **www.cwr.org.uk/store** or call **01252 784700**.
Also available in Christian bookshops.

 Print subscription available

 **Large Print subscription** available

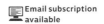 **Email subscription** available

The bestselling *Cover to Cover* Bible Study Series

1 Corinthians
Growing a Spirit-filled church
ISBN: 978-1-85345-374-8

Acts 1–12
Church on the move
ISBN: 978-1-85345-574-2

Elisha
A lesson in faithfulness
ISBN: 978-1-78259-494-9

2 Corinthians
Restoring harmony
ISBN: 978-1-85345-551-3

Acts 13–28
To the ends of the earth
ISBN: 978-1-85345-592-6

Ephesians
Claiming your inheritance
ISBN: 978-1-85345-229-1

1 Peter
Good reasons for hope
ISBN: 978-1-78259-088-0

Barnabas
Son of encouragement
ISBN: 978-1-85345-911-5

Esther
For such a time as this
ISBN: 978-1-85345-511-7

2 Peter
Living in the light of God's promises
ISBN: 978-1-78259-403-1

Bible Genres
Hearing what the Bible really says
ISBN: 978-1-85345-987-0

Fruit of the Spirit
Growing more like Jesus
ISBN: 978-1-85345-375-5

1 Timothy
*Healthy churches –
effective Christians*
ISBN: 978-1-85345-291-8

Daniel
Living boldly for God
ISBN: 978-1-85345-986-3

Galatians
Freedom in Christ
ISBN: 978-1-85345-648-0

David
A man after God's own heart
ISBN: 978-1-78259-444-4

God's Rescue Plan
*Finding God's fingerprints
on human history*
ISBN: 978-1-85345-294-9

23rd Psalm
The Lord is my shepherd
ISBN: 978-1-85345-449-3

Ecclesiastes
*Hard questions and
spiritual answers*
ISBN: 978-1-85345-371-7

Great Prayers of the Bible
Applying them to our lives today
ISBN: 978-1-85345-253-6

2 Timothy and Titus
Vital Christianity
ISBN: 978-1-85345-338-0

Abraham
Adventures of faith
ISBN: 978-1-78259-089-7

Elijah
A man and his God
ISBN: 978-1-85345-575-9

Hebrews
Jesus – simply the best
ISBN: 978-1-85345-337-3

Hosea
The love that never fails
ISBN: 978-1-85345-290-1

Isaiah 1-39
Prophet to the nations
ISBN: 978-1-85345-510-0

Isaiah 40-66
Prophet of restoration
ISBN: 978-1-85345-550-6

James
Faith in action
ISBN: 978-1-85345-293-2

Jeremiah
The passionate prophet
ISBN: 978-1-85345-372-4

John's Gospel
Exploring the seven miraculous signs
ISBN: 978-1-85345-295-6

Joseph
The power of forgiveness and reconciliation
ISBN: 978-1-85345-252-9

Joshua 1-10
Hand in hand with God
ISBN: 978-1-78259-542-7

Judges 1-8
The spiral of faith
ISBN: 978-1-85345-681-7

Judges 9-21
Learning to live God's way
ISBN: 978-1-85345-910-8

Luke
A prescription for living
ISBN: 978-1-78259-270-9

Mark
Life as it is meant to be lived
ISBN: 978-1-85345-233-8

Mary
The mother of Jesus
ISBN: 978-1-78259-402-4

Moses
Face to face with God
ISBN: 978-1-85345-336-6

Names of God
Exploring the depths of God's character
ISBN: 978-1-85345-680-0

Nehemiah
Principles for life
ISBN: 978-1-85345-335-9

Parables
Communicating God on earth
ISBN: 978-1-85345-340-3

Philemon
From slavery to freedom
ISBN: 978-1-85345-453-0

Philippians
Living for the sake of the gospel
ISBN: 978-1-85345-421-9

Prayers of Jesus
Hearing His heartbeat
ISBN: 978-1-85345-647-3

Proverbs
Living a life of wisdom
ISBN: 978-1-85345-373-1

Revelation 1-3
Christ's call to the Church
ISBN: 978-1-85345-461-5

Revelation 4-22
The Lamb wins! Christ's final victory
ISBN: 978-1-85345-411-0

Rivers of Justice
Responding to God's call to righteousness today
ISBN: 978-1-85345-339-7

Ruth
Loving kindness in action
ISBN: 978-1-85345-231-4

The Armour of God
Living in His strength
ISBN: 978-1-78259-583-0

The Beatitudes
Immersed in the grace of Christ
ISBN: 978-1-78259-495-6

The Covenants
God's promises and their relevance today
ISBN: 978-1-85345-255-0

The Creed
Belief in action
ISBN: 978-1-78259-202-0

The Divine Blueprint
God's extraordinary power in ordinary lives
ISBN: 978-1-85345-292-5

The Holy Spirit
Understanding and experiencing Him
ISBN: 978-1-85345-254-3

The Image of God
His attributes and character
ISBN: 978-1-85345-228-4

The Kingdom
Studies from Matthew's Gospel
ISBN: 978-1-85345-251-2

The Letter to the Romans
Good news for everyone
ISBN: 978-1-85345-250-5

The Lord's Prayer
Praying Jesus' way
ISBN: 978-1-85345-460-8

The Prodigal Son
Amazing grace
ISBN: 978-1-85345-412-7

The Second Coming
Living in the light of Jesus' return
ISBN: 978-1-85345-422-6

The Sermon on the Mount
Life within the new covenant
ISBN: 978-1-85345-370-0

Thessalonians
Building Church in changing times
ISBN: 978-1-78259-443-7

The Ten Commandments
Living God's Way
ISBN: 978-1-85345-593-3

The Uniqueness of our Faith
What makes Christianity distinctive?
ISBN: 978-1-85345-232-1

For current prices or to order, visit **www.cwr.org.uk/store**
Available online or from Christian bookshops.

SmallGroup central

All of our small group ideas and resources in one place

Online:

www.smallgroupcentral.org.uk
is filled with free video teaching,
tools, articles and a whole host
of ideas.

On the road:

A range of seminars themed for
small groups can be brought to
your local community. Contact us at
hello@smallgroupcentral.org.uk

In print:

Books, study guides and DVDs
covering an extensive list of themes,
Bible books and life issues.

Log on and find out more at:
www.smallgroupcentral.org.uk

Courses and events

Waverley Abbey College

Publishing and media

Conference facilities

Transforming lives

CWR's vision is to enable people to experience personal transformation through applying God's Word to their lives and relationships.

Our Bible-based training and resources help people around the world to:
- Grow in their walk with God
- Understand and apply Scripture to their lives
- Resource themselves and their church
- Develop pastoral care and counselling skills
- Train for leadership
- Strengthen relationships, marriage and family life and much more.

Our insightful writers provide daily Bible reading notes and other resources for all ages, and our experienced course designers and presenters have gained an international reputation for excellence and effectiveness.

CWR's Training and Conference Centres in Surrey and East Sussex, England, provide excellent facilities in idyllic settings – ideal for both learning and spiritual refreshment.

CWR Applying God's Word
to everyday life and relationships

CWR, Waverley Abbey House,
Waverley Lane, Farnham,
Surrey GU9 8EP, UK

Telephone: **+44 (0)1252 784700**
Email: **info@cwr.org.uk**
Website: **www.cwr.org.uk**

Registered Charity No. 294387
Company Registration No. 1990308